A Drive Through Time:
Carriages, Horses and History

First Publish Date 2006
Copyright © 2014 by Equine Heritage Institute, Inc.

All rights reserved. No part of this publication may be reproduced, distributed, or transmitted in any form or by any means, including photocopying, recording, or other electronic or mechanical methods, without the prior written permission of the publisher, except in the case of brief quotations embodied in critical reviews and certain other noncommercial uses permitted by copyright law. For permission requests, write to the publisher, addressed "Attention: Permissions Coordinator," at the address below.

Gloria Austin Carriage Collection, LLC
Equine Heritage Institute, Inc.
3024 Marion County Road
Weirsdale, FL 32195
(352) 753-2826 Office
(3520753-6186 Fax

Ordering Information:
Quantity sales; Special discounts are available on quantity purchases by corporations, associations, and others. For details, contact the publisher at the address above.

Printed in the United States of America

ISBN 978-1499176988

First Edition

Special Thanks to:

Gloria Austin
Earle Billington
Linda Beaulieu
Charley Hammock
David Saunders
Bonnie Roof
Melissa Warner
Charon Bogner
Joe Bongiovanni
Michelle Dlugoborski
Kacy Tipton-Fashik
Teresa and Bob Wooddy
Amy, Renee, and Jordan Golisano

Gloria Austin Carriage Collection, LLC
Equine Heritage Institute, Inc.
3024 Marion County Road
Weirsdale, FL 32195
(352) 753-2826 Office
(3520753-6186 Fax

www.gloriaaustin.com
www.equineheritagemuseum.com
www.equineheritageinstitute.org

THE HORSE	7
THE WHEEL	8
CARRIAGE AND HARNESS COMPONENTS	9
TYPES OF TURNOUT	10
CARRIAGE LAMPS	11
THE CHARIOT	12
THE SEDAN CHAIR	13
THE TIKKER	14
THE SICILIAN CARETTA	15
THE TRAVELING COACH	16
THE BODY BREAK	17
THE BREAK-DE-CHASSE	18
THE TANDEM CART	19
THE CHAR-A-BANC	20
THE WAGONETTE	21
THE PONY GOVERNESS CART	22
THE PARK DRAG	23
THE TOUR DE LAC	24
RESTORING HISTORY:	25
THE DRESS CHARIOT	25
THE SOCIABLE	27
THE GOAT SOCIABLE	28
THE CALECHE	29
THE BROUGHAM	30
THE CLARENCE	31
THE VICTORIA	32
THE HANSOM CAB	33
THE CABRIOLET	34
THE PHAETON	35
THE BASKET-BODY PHAETON	36
THE ROAD CART	37
THE JENNY LIND	38
THE GODDARD BUGGY	39
THE PRAIRIE SCHOONER	40
THE CONCORD STAGE COACH	41
THE CHUCK WAGON	42
THE SULKY	43

THE PORTLAND CUTTER	44
THE GERMANTOWN COUPE ROCKAWAY	45
THE MILK WAGON	46
THE OIL WAGON	47
THE PEDDLER'S WAGON	48
THE U.S. MAIL CART	49
FIRE HORSES	50
THE HOSE CARRIAGE	51
PENTA FIRE PUMPER	52
U.S. ARMY SUPPLY WAGON	53
THE UNSUNG HEROES OF WORLD WAR I	54
THE OMNIBUS	56
THE BLACK AUTOMOBILE	57
THE 1928 ROLLS ROYCE	58
GLOSSARY OF TERMS	59
BIBLIOGRAPHY	61

This page intentionally left blank

The Horse

There have been approximately six thousand years of history with the horse for transportation compared to that of one hundred years of history with the automobile. The horse was first harnessed around 2300 BC as a weapon of war in the hands of charioteers. The lands that they conquered would be forever altered, and the horse was engendered as a symbol of power and prestige.

As our societies progressed, the use of horses broadened from conquering war heroes, to our main mode of transportation for thousands of years to come. They transported culture by moving people, goods, messages, ideas, language, and technology. They pulled our history along by bringing progress and shrinking the vastness of a large and unforgiving world. Without them, our world would be a much different place. Men may have made history, but they did so on the backs of the horses that they rode or drove.

After thousands of years of dedicated service, the horse was replaced in roughly a thirty-year time span, by the development of the automobile. Thousands of years of heritage, tradition, and culture were replaced and forgotten in less than half a century. Today, less than a full century removed from having a society centered on the horse, only a small fraction of the horses' proud and vital legacy survives and is available to the general population. Most people today have little or no contact with horses. Theirs is a world devoid of a companion, replaced by of a turn of the key, the smell of gasoline, and the shift of a gear.

Yet there still remains remnants of our lost past that are preserved and carried on by a dedicated group of modern enthusiasts. They are dedicated to educating and helping people reconnect with their past. This is the mission of the Equine Heritage Institute and its benefactor, Ms. Gloria Austin. The pages that follow are a glimpse of an era not so long past, an era of horses and wheeled transportation that Ms. Austin has preserved for generations to come, through the Gloria Austin Carriage Collection in Weirsdale, Florida. This book is dedicated to allowing you a glimpse into that past!

The Wheel

The development of the wheel is one of man's greatest inventions. With this development, man was better able to harness the horse and thus revolutionize transportation. Not only could we travel faster, but we could also increase the load to be carried. The average man could carry a load of fifty pounds, a horse can carry an average load of two hundred pounds, but a horse with a wheeled vehicle can pull a load twice his own weight. Thus, a one thousand pound horse can pull a load of two thousand pounds. Overall, we not only maximized the efficiency of travel, but also the amount of goods or supplies that can be moved at any given time.

There are four major components of the wheel: the hub, the spokes, the fellies and the tire. The tire was applied after the initial construction to protect the felloes. This was done by heating an iron loop, pounding it into shape around the wooden rim, and rapidly cooling it with water, causing the iron to shrink around the wooden wheel. All this would have been done by a Wheelwright.

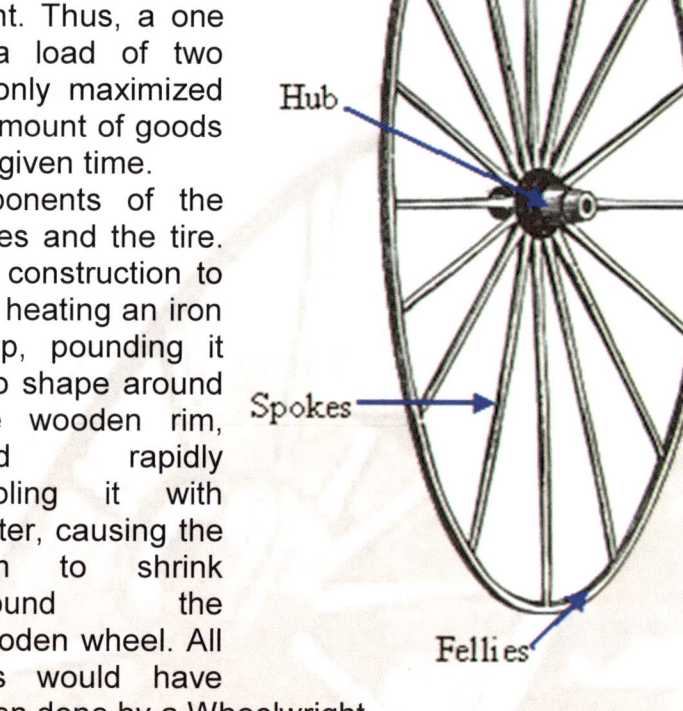

Typically, you can tell the difference between a country vehicle and a city vehicle by the tires. Country vehicles had iron tires, and city vehicles had rubber tires. This was done to help minimize the sound that wheels made as they clattered over paved city streets.

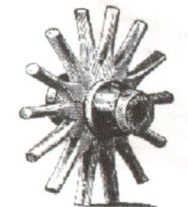

ROUSE BAND WHEEL COMPLETE.

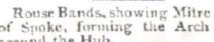 

Rouse Bands, showing Mitre of Spoke, forming the Arch around the Hub.

Interior Construction of the Hub.

Rouse Bands, Flanges and Mortises.

Carriage and Harness Components

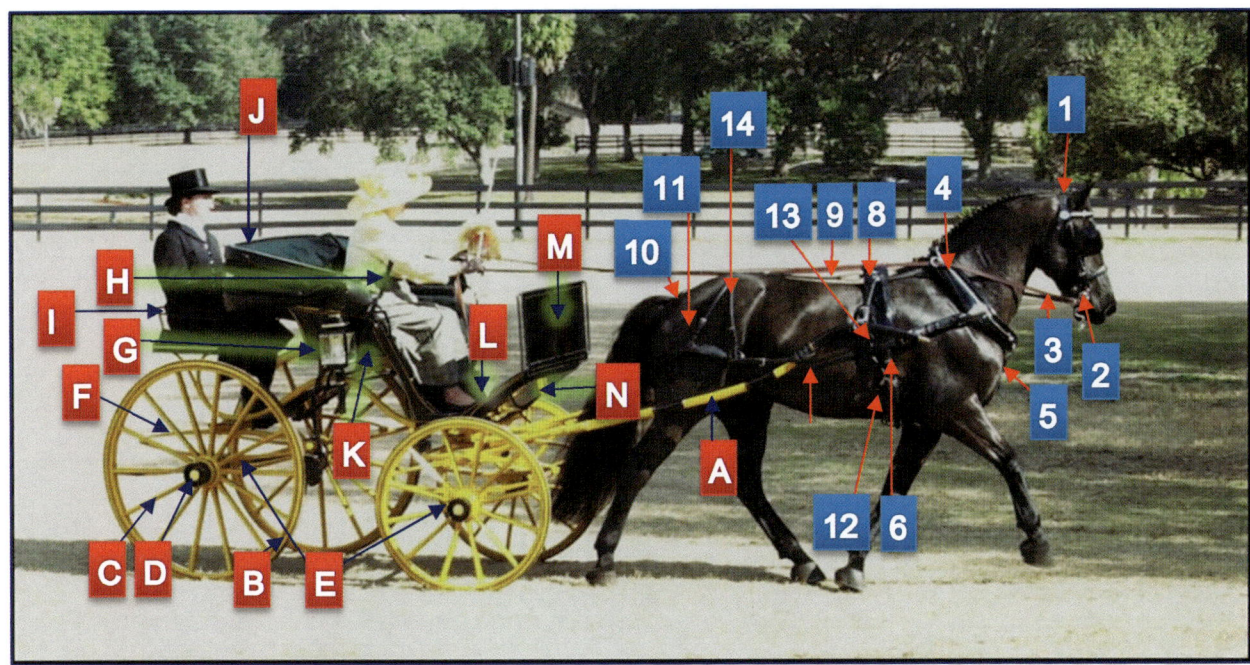

Parts of the Carriage

A. Shaft
B. Wheel
C. Spoke
D. Hu
E. Front & Rear Axles
F. Elliptic Spring
G. Lamp
H. Brake Handle
I. Groom's Seat
J. Hood
K. Body
L. Floor Board
M. Dash Board
N. Toe Board

Parts of the Harness

1. Bridle
2. Bit
3. Reins
4. Neck/Full Collar
5. False Martingale
6. Girth
7. Trace
8. Saddle/Pad
9. Back Strap
10. Crupper
11. Breeching
12. Overgirth/Bellyband
13. Tug
14. Loin Strap

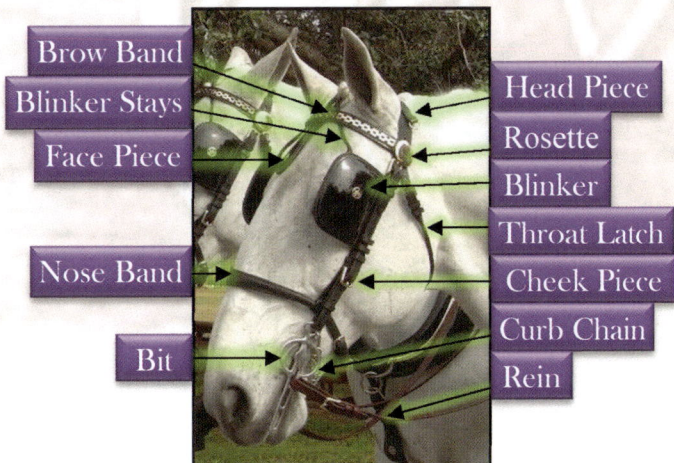

9

Types of Turnout

Single

Pair

Three a Breast   Tandem   Unicorn

Four-in-Hand

Pic-Axe

Carriage Lamps

The use of lamps on carriages served a different function than that of our modern headlights on automobiles. Lamps were used on carriages not for illumination of the road, but for the practical purpose to be seen by other carriages while traveling on the road at night. Toe board or dash board lamps also served as a safety feature so that the driver could see if the reins were twisted or make sure that the bridle and harness were secure. Lamps also took on the role as an indication of social status due in part to the onset of the industrial revolution which allowed for more intricate metalworking and more ornate lamps.

Carriage lamps burned candles, oil, or gas, and came in a variety of sizes, styles and finishes. It is important that the right lamp is selected for the right vehicle. It should be proportionate to the carriage, have the same quality, style, and have a matching metal finish.

The Chariot

The development of the horse drawn chariot revolutionized both warfare and man's relationship with the horse. By harnessing the speed and mobility of the horse, early societies were able to wage war and conquer lands much further away, thus transforming civilizations as old ones fell and new ones emerged. Chariot use was widespread from Ireland to China, and was a dominant military weapon until around 1000 BC, when it was replaced by mounted cavalry.

The utilization of the chariot forever altered the human relationship with the horse. Horses became a symbol of power and prestige, and thus secured themselves as animals to be honored and revered. For centuries to come, the horse remained a symbol of greatness and nobility and men sought to be depicted and remembered astride a horse.

The chariot on this page is a replica of the chariot found in the tomb of the Egyptian pharaoh Tutankhamen, who reigned from 1334-1325 BC. It was originally made for the Henry Ford Museum in the 1920's.

The Sedan Chair

The most likely origin for the name of the sedan chair comes from the Italian word sede or to sit. They were first used in Italy in the sixteenth century and soon spread to other countries. In England, sedan chairs were initially shunned by the general public because they required the use of humans to do the work of animals. Yet public opinion changed and sedan chairs were a popular mode of transportation for private, as well as public transport. They were cheaper than hackney coaches, allowed for indoor transit, and often times were faster than traveling through the crowded streets. They remained a popular mode of transportation up until the 1800's.

This particular chair is a beautiful example of a chair that would have been used by the upper class.

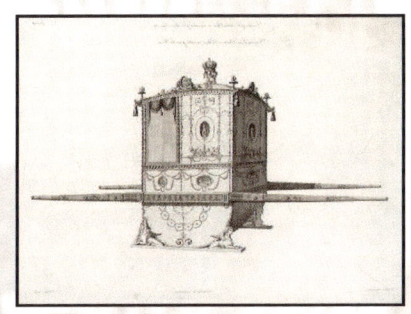

Sedan chairs were carried by two twelve foot long poles which passed through metal brackets affixed to the sides of the chair. The chair would be entered and exited through the front, and carried by two men who supported the load with the assistance of shoulder straps. Often the family's coat of arms would be displayed on the vehicle.

Public sedan chairs for ordinary city dwellers were much plainer in appearance.

The Tikker

The tikker developed out of the Dutch passion for racing their horses on frozen canals in winter. They held only one passenger plus the driver who sat on the rear seat. A light load was desired so that the horse could make a faster time and perform to its best advantage.

Typically a man with his wife seated in front of him, raced the family's prized horse. Dutch horses of native Friesian and Gelderlander breeding are still shown to tikkers which have been family-owned for generations.

This tikker is one of a pair, which was displayed by Count de Hemptinne in the Hotel Particulier in Ghent, Belgium.

The oriental designs stem from the Dutch background as society of worldwide traders. The designs were inspired by the imported porcelain pieces that were used as counter weight aboard returning ships carrying loads of silk and tea.

The Sicilian Caretta

The Sicilian Caretta is an old Italian cart that was popular from the Medieval era through the mid-20th century. The historical use of this cart was for celebrations upon the return of soldiers who went off to battle. This practice began during the times of the crusades.

Sicilian Carettas are very colorful and ornate. The side panels feature a knight returning from battle and a festival being held in his honor.

The body and wheels contain rich carvings of faces and heads of people. The harness is equally decorative and adorned with colorful stones, glass, and plumes. Many were lined with scented leather and expensive textiles.

The Traveling Coach

Dating from the early 1800's this coach was used for long distance travel before the advent of the railroads. Traveling coaches were luxurious vehicles typically used by the nobility and their families.

This one seats two persons facing forward with room for two seated backwards. The seats can be made into a bed where two occupants can stretch out their legs under the driver's seat to offer the possibility of a night's sleep, as accommodations at inns and post houses were generally poor. The shutters can be used to shade the occupants from daylight as well as offer the occupants more privacy.

This vehicle has a driver's seat, but these coaches were often driven postillion as to allow more room for luggage and cargo. Teams of horses would be hired and changed out along the way at inns or stage stops.

The Body Break
The Wagonette Break

Body Break was the English term associated with this particular large carriage that was used to transport both people and cargo. In the United States the body break was known as a Wagonette Break.

This type of vehicle was popular with the military and educational institutions since it could take a large number of people from places such as the train station to barracks or dormitories. The seats can be folded down for a return trip to pick up luggage.

The Break-de-Chasse

This is the only carriage that carries both English and French words in its title. The English term break meant a four-wheeled passenger vehicle with an elevated driver's seat. De Chasse which means "of the chase," indicates that this break was driven to the hunt. The hunting hounds were carried in the body of the carriage.

The passengers sat atop, and the multi-seating capacity allowed for both hunters and their staff to traverse the countryside in search of game.

The Tandem Cart

As evidenced by its picture, this tandem cart has such superior balance that it can actually stand alone without the aid of the shaft stand. This feat is achieved by sliding the box to the center of the four irons which support it.

Balance was important to keep the weight of the shafts from becoming too heavy over the horse's back. As many as four people can ride comfortably on this two-wheeled carriage, and as many as six hunting hounds can fit in the crate underneath.

In a Hunting Tandem, the lead horse would wear his saddle and be ready to be ridden when the driver arrived at the designated field. A groom would rest the driven horse and have him ready for a return trip to the owner's residence when the hunt was over.

This example from Jennifer Singleton's blog, the Slower Road from the CAA 2011 pleasure show of Duke and Dante as a sporting tandem you can see the lead horse has his riding tack on and is in an open bridle.

The Char-a-Banc

The Char-a-Banc, which means a car with benches, originated in France in the early 1840's and was modeled after the Swiss national carriage. It soon arrived in England when one was presented to Queen Victoria by King Louis Philippe as a gift. It was primarily a country vehicle that was used by large establishments as a convenient method to transport larger groups of people and luggage, as in the event of a shooting party. It also served as a vehicle for young or inexperienced drivers to learn how to drive teams of horses due to its road-holding qualities. In time, this vehicle became more associated as a tourist vehicle.

Char-a-Bancs are pulled by four horses, and due to their height, passengers would climb aboard by folding stairs. A canopy could be used to protect passengers from the elements and a variety of seating arrangements were available. This Char-a-Banc can seat eight, with the two benches in the center facing each other.

One interesting feature about this particular Char-a-Banc is the step attached to the friction brakes on the back wheels. The driver would operate the brakes with a hand lever, but if extra braking power was needed to hold back the weight of the carriage, the grooms seated in the rear could "ride the brake" as well.

The Wagonette

Built in Paris, France in the late 1800's, this lovely example of a wagonette can be driven to a pair or a four-in-hand of fairly light-weight horses. The vehicle is entered from a step at the rear of the carriage, and passengers sit on bench seats facing one another. Some models had hinged seats that could be dropped flat against the side of the vehicle if cargo instead of passengers was to be transported.

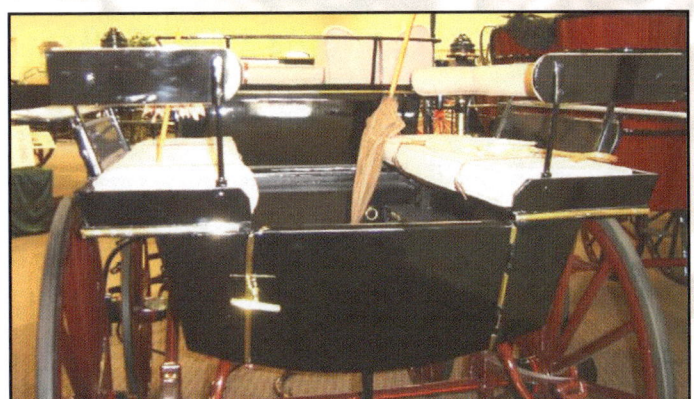

Almost every wealthy household of the nineteenth century had a wagonette to transport servants from summer to winter homes. The wagonette was the "maid of all work," for large households and hotels alike. They were used for picnics, sporting trips, station taxis, and for club outings.

The Pony Governess Cart

Large numbers of these carts were built to be used by the governess of a household to take the children on excursions. The body shape was that of a tub which was designed to keep children safe from wheels and hooves if the pony suddenly lunged forward. The door handle was placed rather low on the exterior and thus out of the reach of tiny hands. The enclosed body protects children from falling out of the vehicle or getting caught in the wheel.

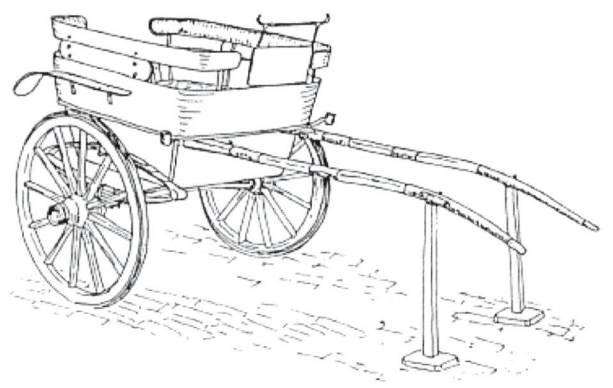

Another safety feature taken is ensuring a better center of gravity by hanging the body between a pair of elliptic springs on a cranked axle. This helps to prevent the possibility of the vehicle turning over.

The Park Drag

The Park Drag is a lighter version of the road coach. They have a refined finish and are often painted the colors of the family who owned them.

The back of the coach can be folded down to form a table and is used to serve food and refreshments. The built in wooden compartments, called cellerettes, store items such as china, crystal, iced foods, libations, and linens. The inside is fully upholstered and some even have a toilet inside.

Tailgate Picnic

Park Drags were built for gentlemen who wanted to drive their four-in-hand for leisure purposes. They were driven to the park for picnics or to sporting events such as race meets and polo matches. The height of the coach with the seats atop made it an ideal place to watch events and the coach therefore served as a mobile grandstand.

The Tour de Lac

The Tour de Lac is a unique vehicle that was primarily developed for sightseeing tourists in the Swiss and Italian Alps. It was drawn by a large pony who would have been hand led by a handler as tourists enjoyed the view of mountains or lakes.

The seat, which was set to the left side, allowed for a comfortable and uninhibited scenic view. The vehicle itself was well suited for the mountain trails due to its small tracking.

Another use that developed for the Tour de Lac was that of an observation vehicle for officers. While observing or inspecting troops, the officer could comfortably sit and view the troops that were to be inspected while marching or presenting.

Restoring History:

The Golden Chariot

While traveling in Oregon, Ms. Austin came upon an old, rotting and dilapidated carriage. As she examined the vehicle, she noticed that it was a dress chariot that would have been used by royalty. Further examination of the hubs revealed that it was a rare Armbruster Dress Chariot.

Its history began in Austria sometime between 1840 and 1860. It was used by Emperor Franz Joseph and his royal court for special occasions that required an elegant formal coach. The vehicle had been brought to the United States by the movie industry, and used in the 1937 film, The Prisoner of Zenda. From that point it had fallen into the poor condition that it was in when Ms. Austin discovered and purchased it in 1998.

From that point, the golden chariot traveled by truck to the east coast, secured in a sea-land container, and was loaded aboard a ship to travel across the Atlantic Ocean to Belgium for a complete restoration by Patrick Schroven. It would take eighteen months of dedicated labor to breathe life back into a classic and timeless piece of history.

To the knowledge of most European museum directors, it is one of only two remaining Armbruster Dress Chariots left in the world. One resides at the Kremlin, and the other resides here in the Gloria Austin Collection.

The Dress Chariot

Made by the coachbuilder Armbruster in the early 1840's for Emperor Franz Joseph of Austria, this wonderful ceremonial vehicle was used by the Royal Family as they traveled about the streets of Vienna to greet their constituents.

The stunning hammercloth over the driver's seat is of silk velvet, decorated with two hundred and ten hand turned and covered gold bullions. Over one hundred and fifty meters of gold cables further adorn the cloth. The great seal of the Austrian Empire superimposed with the personal crest of the Hapsburg family completes the presentation.

The vehicle seats two occupants, facing forward. There are no handles on the doors' interior, and communication with the coachman was via a pull string attached to a button on the back of his coat. Footmen walked beside or stood on the platform at the rear of the vehicle and were ready to assist the Royals as they entered or exited the vehicle. Steps fold down from the interior for entry.

The Sociable

This late 19th century sociable would have been coachman driven to a flashy pair of matched horses with the box seat higher than the passenger seats.

Sociables, according to 18th century coachbuilder William Felton, gained their name from the fact that they could easily accommodate an entire family for outings. It was also ideal for a gentleman's use in the park or for transporting the household staff from city to country houses.

The carriage was entered by folding steps, and passengers sat facing one another. If only two passengers rode inside, the front seatback was folded down. In the case of inclement weather, a rain hood could be unfolded from the seatback to cover passengers on that seat.

The Goat Sociable

This lovely little vehicle was actually used to transport the infants and toddlers of wealthy aristocrats. It would be put to a well-trained goat which would be led by a household servant or driven by a precocious child. In this way, the young lad would learn his first lessons in handling the reins and driving a vehicle. It also served as an entertainment means and kept children occupied.

Like other sociables in the collection, this scaled-down version has seating for at least four, and can be entered from either side of the vehicle behind the driver's seat. Those seated on the rear seat had the protection of a folding hood.

The Caleche

This elegant town carriage required the service of well-schooled postilion riders able to handle the high spirited and superb horses needed to match the grandeur of the formal work to which it was put.

One groom in full livery rides on the seat behind, ready to assist the passengers entering or leaving the vehicle.

The lovely silk brocade upholstered seats accommodate four passengers sitting vis-à-vis, or facing one another. If only two passengers are riding, the back of the front seat folds downward to protect the interior. A substantial hood covers the occupants of the rear seat and can be folded down when weather permits.

The Brougham

The original Brougham was designed by Lord Brougham and built by Messrs Robinson and Cook of London in 1838. Its development stemmed from Lord Brougham's desire for a more suitable gentleman's carriage that was more elegant and glorified than that of general street cabs. Many had a luxurious interior design, and were outfitted with ashtrays, clocks, mirrors, reading lamps, looking glasses, and card pockets. They were the Mercedes Benz of their time.

The Brougham was a coachman-driven carriage that could be driven by either a single horse or a pair. Due to the fact that the passenger was separate from the driver, communication was accomplished through a tubular whistle that hung in the interior of the carriage. A system of long and short whistles would indicate to the driver whether to turn left or right, stop, go, or return home.

The Clarence

Like the Brougham, the Clarence is a coachman-driven vehicle, but a larger vehicle that can seat four people. It was sometimes referred to as the Growler due to the noise it made as it traveled down the road. They were used as both private and commercial high class vehicles, and are still employed by the Royal Mews to this day.

The Clarence was typically pulled by a pair of horses. Like most carriages, blankets for the horses would be carried in the boot under the coachman's seat if the weather was cold. A footman would ride next to the coachman to assist the passengers when entering or exiting the vehicle.

The Victoria

Thought to have originated in England, the Victoria was an elegant coachman driven vehicle that became popular in the late 1800's. Its widespread popularity was a result of its favorability with Queen Victoria while she was still Princess.

The Victoria came in numerous designs. It could be open with vis-à-vis seating for up to four people or accommodate two people facing forward. They could also be constructed to be pulled by either a single horse or a pair of horses or ponies. The driver's seat on most Victorias is removable so that the vehicle could be postilion driven. The back was often fitted with an Urchin bar to prevent children from hitching a ride on the back of the carriage as it was being driven through city streets.

Many women desired to travel in the Victoria to social gatherings or shopping trips due to its comfortable accommodations such as the seats and springs. This particular Victoria has a double suspension of both elliptic and cee springs for ultimate comfort. It also contains a smaller removable seat for children located on the back side of the dash.

The Hansom Cab

The Hansom Cab is named for its early designer, Mr. J.A. Hansom, but cabs used for public transport in the latter half of the 19th century bear little resemblance to earlier models.

The driver sits high above at the rear of the box for a better view of the city. An unusually strong and quiet cab horse was required to pull the vehicle because the shaft weight was extremely heavy.

At rest, the driver would release the "spoke" under the carriage and ask the horse to back a few steps, using the same principle as a kickstand. This would help to take some of the carriage weight off the horses back and save him for further work.

The Cabriolet

A vehicle of great popularity with young, unmarried men in the 1800's, the Cabriolet was originally imported from France and greatly improved in design by Count D'Orsay. The hood protected the driver and his passenger from inclement weather and prying eyes. An apron of wood or leather would add further protection across the legs. The curved shafts dropped low at the rear end, allowing easy access into the vehicle.
The possession of a Cabriolet became a status symbol and demanded a bold horse of great quality and showy action. The great front-end weight of the carriage did not lend itself to long distance travel and tended to bounce along the city streets. An additional feature of this turnout was a bell, which hung from the horse's collar. The vehicle was frequently used after dark and traveled at considerable speed and the bell was a warning to other travelers of its approach.

Many cabriolets provided a padded platform between the rear springs for a servant to stand on while the gentleman drove. The lack of such a platform on this vehicle might indicate that the owner was beyond his "wild oats" years and used the vehicle for general daytime transportation. As a public conveyance, the Cabriolet preceded the Hansom Cab.

The Phaeton

Photo by Robert Jennings

Photo by Robert Jennings

Phaetons are a light and swift group of four-wheeled carriages that come in many sizes and styles. While lighter than the average four wheeled vehicle they tend to be safer and more comfortable than two wheeled vehicles. The common factor between all Phaetons is that they are owner driven, which allows the owner the satisfaction of driving his own horses and carriage. During the height of the carriage years the phaeton became immensely popular as a sporting, pleasure, and exercise vehicle.

Photos by Robert Jennings

Photo by Robert Miska

The name Phaeton is derived from the Greek mythology and the myth of Phaethon. Phaethon was the son of Helios, the sun god, who drove the Chariot of the Sun so recklessly that Zeus struck him down with a thunderbolt, fearing that he would scorch the earth.

Photo by Robert Jennings

The Basket-Body Phaeton

    This vehicle's body is similar in shape to the Queen-body sleigh which was named for Queen Victoria. This carriage was popular with the modern women of the day, who enjoyed this design because it permitted easy entry and roominess for long skirts. Americans used the natural materials and skills available to them in their carriage building, and the wicker industry flourished in the heyday of the carriage era.

    Basket carriages were generally intended for summertime use, and the parasol top gave protection from the sun. The tan colored upholstery and parasol fabric made the dust of the summer roadways less noticeable.

    An interesting feature of this vehicle is that the ironwork and undercarriage are painted and hand grained to simulate woodwork, a fashionable practice of the early 1900's, not unlike our modern day "antiquing" methods. The ironwork of the carriage would be said to have a "faux" finish.

The Road Cart

With seating for two people, this cart is perfect for a young man to "go a courting" on a summer evening or for a mother and child to make a trek to the market together. The simplest of vehicles, it was produced in vast quantities and often sold mail order. The Sears and Roebuck catalog of the early 1900's lists several road carts for under $10.00.

Today, original examples of road carts are difficult to find because of the multiple uses to which they were put by their owners and the fact that they were usually left out in the elements.

The Jenny Lind

In 1850, showman Phineas T. Barnum, the great impresario and inventor of modern mass marketing, persuaded the soprano Jenny Lind to come from her home in Sweden and tour the U.S. He created a frenzy of popular enthusiasm for the so-called "Swedish Nightingale," making Jenny Lind as famous in her day as Elvis or The Beatles are in ours.

Barnum's primary motivation for promoting Jenny Lind was financial. Without her permission, he licensed Jenny Lind merchandise from bonnets to boots, hair gloss to tobacco, and even the items of spindled furniture which bear her name to this day. Ms. Lind, however, sang for a higher purpose and devoted herself to charity and gave most of her earnings away. The two personalities collided, and much has been written in opera and prose about the tumultuous relationship. Whether Miss Lind approved or not, the carriage has been named for her.

The Goddard Buggy

(The Doctor's Phaeton)

The Goddard Buggy or Doctor's Phaeton was commonly used by doctors who made house calls. Like today, a doctor's job is never off the clock, many doctors would work around the clock if his services were needed. Inclement weather was dealt with by the extension top and a cotton oil rain cover that folds out from the dashboard. These doctors relied on a dependable, well-mannered horse that could be relied upon to find the way home if the doc dozed off on the drive home.

The Prairie Schooner

Covered wagons such as the Prairie Schooner derived their name from their large white canvas tops that resembled a ship's sails. They first came into prominence during the gold rush age of the 1840's when thousands of Americans packed up their lives and went in search of new ones.

The journey that they embarked on was a harsh and dangerous trip. Trail discipline was hard to enforce and it was a constant battle against the elements. The two thousand miles from Missouri to California had to be made in a five month window, or else risk succumbing to the seasons and weather. To cover fifteen miles a day was a good strong pace, and a swollen river could delay a wagon train for two or more weeks.

The wagons themselves were heavy, difficult to maneuver, and always in need of repair. Wagons were typically pulled by oxen or mules, and the loss of a draft animal could leave the wagon stranded in its tracks. Yet despite these hardships, people packed up what little they could and migrated west in the hopes of a better life and the fulfillment of Manifest Destiny.

The Concord Stage Coach

As Americans pushed westward, they looked for better and faster ways to cover the vast distance that existed between Missouri and California. Prior to the arrival of the railroad, the only way to get there was by boat, wagon train, or the stagecoach. By 1860, the overland stage coach was the primary means of land transportation between Missouri and the west coast. It took approximately twenty days to cover the two thousand mile trek that was a jammed packed, uncomfortable, and dangerous journey.

Due to the fact that the roads were rough and rugged, the typical English coaches would eventually smash to pieces. An innovative design was perfected by Abbott and Downing which used the system of leather thorough braces, which allowed the coach box to sway much like a hammock as the vehicle bounced along. This design was so successful that the Abbott and Downing Company was soon exporting coaches to South Africa, New Zealand, Australia, and anywhere else that roads were virtually non-existent.

The Chuck Wagon

The chuck wagon served as the center of life itself for cowhands while driving large herds of cattle on the range. They relied on the chuck wagon and the "cookie" for all of their provisions and needs while on the range. The wagon cook had the tough job of not only preparing all the meals, but he would have also served as the barber, doctor, banker, mediator, and whatever else was required of him. They had to keep ahead of the herd and have camp and meals ready by the time the men caught up.

The tradition of chuck wagons developed after the Civil War. In the early days of cattle drives, cowhands had to pack and carry with them all the supplies that they needed.

Rancher Charles Goodnight can be credited with developing the first chuck wagon when he converted an army supply wagon for trail use by building a stronger wagon box and adding a chuck box at the rear. The wagon also had iron axles and wider wheels for better traction and durability in rugged terrain. Typically, chuck wagons were pulled by teams of four mules or horses.

The Sulky

Said to have been favored by people who prefer their own company, or those having fits of sulking, these vehicles have forward-facing seating for only one person. They were almost always used by men, which earned the sulky the nickname of a "selfish" from disgruntled American women. They are also used for trotting and pacing races.

This sulky belonged to the harness racing hall of fame trotter Lou Dillon. She was the first trotter in history to cover a mile in less than two minutes, recorded at Memphis in 1903. This vehicle comes to the Equine Heritage Institute through the generosity of Mr. Bruce Milligan.

The Portland Cutter

As leisure time became more available, the need arose for a transport which could navigate the snow and ice covered roads, fields and ponds of northern winters. An affordable sleigh, such as the cutter became very popular. They were a light, one-horse sleighs with a single seat for two or three passengers. The best known versions, the Portland and the Albany, were both developed in the early nineteenth century.

Passengers would keep warm using soap stones or foot warmers containing coal or hot water. They also made use of fur-trimmed garments and heavy lap robes. Sleigh bells were employed to alert drivers of other traffic on the roads.

The Germantown Coupe Rockaway

The Germantown Coupe Rockaway is a smaller version of the standard size Rockaway. Rockaways were built in many different styles and came with a variety of names. They were a distinctively American vehicle that was popular among families used for both town and country activities. Furthermore, they are considered a representative of democratic people due to the protection given to the driver and the fact that they could be owner or servant driven.

The Rockaway could be pulled by either a single horse in shafts or a pair of horses with a pole. All Rockaways were hung on elliptical springs and most had a storm hood over the driver's seat. Passengers entered from the sides of the vehicle and sat facing forward. The entry steps on the sides were covered by guards that swing away when the door is opened to prevent slipping in foul weather.

The Milk Wagon

The horse drawn milk wagon would have been a familiar sight in towns and cities up until the mid-1950's. Horse drawn milk wagons were cheaper to maintain and operate for local door to door delivery routes than motorized delivery trucks. Due to their efficiency, they had a big resurgence during World War II in order to conserve gasoline and rubber for the war effort.

Most dairies took great pride and care in their horses and equipment. They often times used flashy looking horses and kept their wagons neat, clean, and nicely painted to portray the impression of freshness and cleanliness.

Milk wagon horses knew their routes so well that they did not rely on the driver for commands. The milkmen could leave their wagons, cut through backyards, emerge a few houses down, and find their horse and wagon would be waiting for them. The horses knew when to move on their own, when not to move, and where to turn. Along their routes, these wonderful horses befriended the local neighborhood children, who often times waited for them with lumps of sugar.

The Oil Wagon

    The Oil Wagon was used to deliver different petroleum products to homes and retail stores. The cylindrical tank was divided into compartments, and each section would hold a different product such as oil, kerosene, or axle grease. Each compartment had its own spigot for dispersal. Oil wagons generally had the capacity to hold between three hundred to one thousand gallons. This particular wagon holds approximately one hundred and fifty gallons.

    The petroleum products that these wagons delivered were essential for everyday use. Oils and kerosene were used as fuel for lighting and heat for stoves. Axle grease was needed for the lubrication of vehicles and the mechanical devices that were used in homes or workshops.

The Peddler's Wagon

This wonderfully functional vehicle was used by one of the many Rawleigh product distributors who were successful during the late 1800's and early 1900's. The salesman would drive this wagon through the rural countryside, selling his wares to housewives, farmers and townsfolk.

The "Rawleigh Man" could provide a tonic for a wide variety of human and livestock ills, and would also have numerous household products for everyday use. The items on display are a collection of original containers and catalogs. Many Rawleigh products are still sold and used today.

The U.S. Mail Cart

Local mail routes required the services of a sensible, quiet horse and an agile delivery man. The horse who knew his route needed no prompting as he stopped at each of his designated drops. The delivery man would step off the cart, make his delivery, and cue the horse that it was time to move on by stepping back onto the cart.

The U. S. Postal Service began its rural mail delivery service in 1896. The first delivery wagons that were used belonged to the individual men who drove them. Most mail delivery vehicles were two-wheeled and light-weight to provide a faster mode of transportation at minimal cost. This mail cart was made by Studebaker & Company of New York who later became one of the first manufacturers of automobiles.

Fire Horses

Before the glare of flashing red and white lights and the roar of the fire truck's engine, there was the thrill of galloping horses heroically pulling our cities fire equipment to the scene of the fire. They were our true heroes in harness and distinguished members of the communities that they loyally served in. At a time when horses were considered "mindless machines," fire horses were regarded as equal partners, and viewed as highly intelligent individuals who had unique and diverse personalities by the firemen who took great pride in their four-legged partners.

Fire horses were always stabled behind or next to the fire equipment. Upon the sound of the alarm, the automatic stall doors flew open, and the horses, with no assistance, would take their places at the vehicle to which they were assigned. The driver would then lower the hanging harness on their backs, and with three quick snaps they could be out of the firehouse, oftentimes in as little as ten seconds.

The response time from the time the alarm rang to the arrival on the scene was on average five to six minutes, the same response time as modern fire trucks today. The stations were strategically placed within a two mile radius of each other, which was the mileage that the horses could run pulling the heavy equipment that could weigh as much as five to six thousand pounds.

The era of the fire horse lasted for about seventy-five years. Their services brought a great advancement to firefighting capabilities, and overall saved many lives and properties with their speed, agility, endurance, and dedication. It was a sad farewell the day that motorized engines replaced the noble fire horses. Yet their legacy lives on as a great source of pride for countless fire companies around the world.

The Hose Carriage

This rare example of a hose carriage has four wheels. It made the task of pulling it easier than the more common two-wheeled cart. This vehicle was actually pulled by four men rather than a horse. Before the fire horse became an essential part of the firefighting arsenal, fire departments relied on the volunteer fire fighters to haul the equipment to the scene.

Upon arrival at the scene of a fire, the hose would be pulled over the roller bar at the rear of the vehicle and attached to whatever source of water was available. The re-winding of the hose would take at least three strong men to accomplish: one to keep the wheel moving, one to guide the hose neatly onto the reel, and one to feed the hose to the vehicle. Upon return to the fire house, the hose would be hung from the watchtower to dry. This was an important procedure because the hoses were made from cotton, and would easily mildew.

It was an exhausting task to haul the equipment, fight the fire, and then return to the station. Yet despite the physical exertion it took to pull the equipment, the introduction of the fire horse to do the job was fiercely resisted. Men had their pride, and it was not to be trampled on by a horse. That sentiment was to change when steam engines entered the scene. They were simply too heavy for the men to pull, and the fire horse then gained the ground it needed to evolve as a heroic and endearing figure of firehouses around the world.

Penta Fire Pumper

While most fire pumpers used steam to pump the pressurized water stream needed to fight fires, this Penta fire pumper used gasoline for power instead. It was built in Sweden in 1905, and used a four cylinder engine that was capable of putting out twenty-four horsepower at eight hundred rpm. It has an overhead cam, which did not come to the United States until the 1980's. It was constructed with top shelf machinery and all fasteners had a metric thread. The overall design was that of simplicity so that the pumper would be more reliable and could be repaired in the field if necessary.

Unfortunately, by the time this pumper was built, it was already obsolete. Many fire departments in the area were switching over from horse drawn engines to self-propelled ones. This Penta Pumper sat abandoned in a lot, subject to the elements for years.

Upon its purchase by Gloria Austin, it was carefully, fully restored to working order by Joe Bongiovanni. It took Joe about two years to restore it to its former glory. The engine was completely frozen and everything was meticulously repaired and restored. Thanks to Joe's extraordinary talent, dedication, and hard work, this wonderful piece of engineering innovation and history has been preserved for generations to come.

U.S. Army Supply Wagon
The Escort Wagon

The U.S. Army developed its specifications for a four-mule and six-mule escort wagon during the Mexican War. The army at first contracted with commercial freighters, such as Russell, Majors and Waddell, but found private muleteers and commercial freighters unreliable. The army instituted their own wagon system with the U.S. Quartermaster Corps and perfected the wagon during the Civil War. It carried all manner of army ordnances, food supplies, tents, bedding, and ammunition.

In 1878, the four-mule wagon generally replaced the six- mule type. Their standard load size was around 3000 lbs., but it was not unusual to have loads around 5000 lbs. Although there were attempts to replace the army wagon with a type known as the Combat Wagon during World War I, the attempt was unsuccessful and the wagon continued to be in use until more suitable all terrain motor vehicles were developed.

Contracts to build army wagons were awarded to major wagon makers such as Espenscheid and Studebaker. This particular vehicle was manufactured by the John Deere Company in 1916. Few examples of these wagons remain today. When the Horse Cavalry was disbanded in 1943, these wagons were considered obsolete, and thousands were burned at Ft. Riley, Kansas. The remaining scrap steel was pulled from the ashes to be used to manufacture arms for World War II.

The Unsung Heroes of World War I

World War I marked a significant turning point in the history of warfare. It occurred at a time when nations had experienced an increased growth in population and industries, a large network of roads and railways, and more centralized governments that were able to commit, mobilize, and equip large armies. Both sides were committed to waging total war and were willing to sacrifice a huge portion of their populations and resources for the war effort. New technologies and innovations were utilized to win the war, such as airplanes, tanks, submarines, gas, flamethrowers, and light machine guns. War had entered the modern age of machinery and industrial mobilization. Yet despite the modern machine age and numerous technological advancements, horses and mules still functioned as the backbone for both the Allies and the Central Powers.

Horses and mules delivered supplies to the front line, pulled the artillery, limber, and ambulance wagons, and transported all the supplies and munitions that were needed to sustain the war. They also played a decisive military factor as cavalry mounts in the Middle Eastern campaign. So many horses and mules were required for this monumental effort that more tons of fodder was shipped in to feed them than that of ordnances for the guns. Men were completely dependent on these animals for transporting every supply that was needed to sustain life and battle, and then relied on them to be carried off the battlefield if injured or killed.

The war could not have been won if it was not for the countless millions of horses and mules who served during World War I. Like the men they worked beside, they experienced and suffered from all the same horrors that war has to offer. Close relationships formed between soldiers and animals that were brought together in such a great time of misery. They lived and died together, and the war could not have been won if it were not for these noble animals.

The Unsung Heroes of World War I continued

In the end, more horses and mules were killed than men in World War I. Approximately ten million horses and mules and eight and a half million soldiers died as a result of the Great War. The war took devastating toll on the world's equine population. Yet despite the gallant effort and vital role that these animals played, no one wanted to pay the price to bring the survivors home. The remaining animals were shot, butchered, or sold to locals to live a life of hard labor and neglect. As we remember and honor the sacrifices and ultimate price that soldiers have paid to ensure freedom, we should never forget all the horses, mules, and other animals who served for their countries as well. If we fail to do so, their sacrifices and essential contributions will fade into history.

Goodbye Old Man:
watercolour by Italian artist Fortunino Matania

The Omnibus

The omnibus is the forerunner of our modern public transportation system. They dominated inner-city transportation until the introduction of motorized vehicles. Their basic designs and passenger loads varied. Smaller versions sat up to sixteen passengers, while the larger varieties could accommodate up to thirty passengers. Many were painted a bright yellow like our modern day cabs.

Most omnibuses were hitched to a pair of horses that would make various stops along a twelve mile route. The boarding passengers would pay more to ride inside the vehicle than those who sat outside. There was tremendous competition between rival companies to cover the different routes at the fastest and most convenient pace.

The Black Automobile

The advent of the horseless carriage meant big changes in the way we moved from one place to another. Carriage manufacturers needed to decide if they were going to continue making horse-drawn vehicles or if they were going to change with the times.

This is a wonderful early example of how a horse carriage was transformed into an early automobile. The box and seat of the vehicle look like a runabout carriage. The steering wheel of the vehicle is positioned on the right side, the same side that was traditionally used to drive a horse.

It was Henry Ford who was credited with the idea of putting the steering wheel on the left side, thus moving the gear shift to the center of the floor board, which provided easier access to the vehicle from either side.

The 1928 Rolls Royce

The transition to the automobile brought the end of the horse and carriage era, and carriage builders the world over had to make a decision to either change with the times or go out of business. The Brewster Company, America's premier builder of coaches and carriages, was no exception.

For a time, Brewster held its own in this new endeavor; but the company was eventually purchased by Rolls Royce of England.

This beautiful automobile bears the names of both companies; as its body was made by Brewster of New York, and its undercarriage and motor were made in England by Rolls.

Glossary of Terms

coachman- one of the highest ranking members of the household staff, who drives the carriages of a wealthy family. Today a coachman takes care not only the horses, their training, and travel arrangements but would be responsible for the truck and transportation of the carriage horses and staff.

dashboard- a board, perpendicular to the ground, made of wood or leather that is located in front of the driver and front passenger's legs in a carriage. It serves to protect them from the dirt and dust kicked up by the horses' feet. Commonly found on runabouts and phaetons.

hackney coach- a horse-drawn vehicle that operated much like the modern day taxi cab. They first made their appearance in London in the early seventeenth century. Soon after, their popularity exploded, and caused major traffic jams throughout the narrow city streets, especially when they traveled at a slow pace hoping to pick up fares. The government combated these problems by passing laws and ordinances, and distributing a set number of licenses for operating within the city. Governed by city ordinances and licensure, a carriage or coach for hire is deemed a cab

lap robe- a blanket that is placed over the calves, knees, and thighs of the driver and passengers to protect their clothing from dirt and dust.

lead horse- the horse or horses that are located in the front of the team.

livery- type of clothing and dress worn by the outdoor household staff who care for the horses and carriages of a wealthy person. Either full (formal) or stable (casual), the color of the jacket was often representative of the household colors. Often times the color of the outfit was coordinated with the color of the carriage.

pole- the pole is located in between the horses. The horses are harnessed to the pole, which allows for the steering and holding back of the carriage. Pole straps connected to the harness of the horses allow for the steering and holding back of the carriage.

postilion- a method of driving a horse in which the driver sits on the ride horse(near horse) and directs the hand horse (off horse) with a single rein and a postillion whip as a means of control versus sitting on the carriage. This allowed privacy to the passengers, and extra space for luggage or goods.

reins- the means through which the horse is driven. It is through the reins that the horse and carriage are steered and stopped. They are made of leather so in case of an emergency, they can break or be cut. They are also almost always brown due to the fact black leather dyes can stain clothing. Reins are one of the means by which the driver communicates with the horse for steering and stopping. The voice and whip are also viewed as aides.

shafts- the two pieces of wood running along the sides of the horse in which a single horse is harnessed to a carriage. They serve as the means of balance, steering, and braking for the carriage.

springs- the suspension systems for carriages. Examples of which are Cee, Telegraph, French Platform, Dennet, Tilbury, and Elliptic springs.

team- the four horses that are put to large phaetons, brakes, and coaches.

toe board- a platform for the feet of a carriage driver which protrudes from the floor board at an approximate 45 degree angle. This coupled with an wedge (angled) seat cushion places the driver of multiple horses in a better position to use his or her body to control horses through the use of the reins.

wheel horse- the horses that are located the closest to the wheels of the carriage. They exert the most effort in pulling the carriage.

Bibliography

Berkebile, Don H. Carriage Terminology: An Historical Dictionary. (Washington: Smithsonian Institution Press, 1979).

Doughty, Robert A. et al. American Military History and the Evolution of Warfare in the Western World. (Lexington: D.C. Heath and Company, 1996).

Duffy, Michael. "The Forgotten Army." First World War.Com: The War to End All Wars. http://www.firstworldwar.com/features/forgottenarmy.htm.

Dunlop, Richard. Wheels West 1590-1900. (Chicago: Rand McNally, 1977).

Fox, Charles Phillip. Horses in Harness. (Greendale: Reiman Associates, Inc., 1987).

Working Horses. (Whitewater: Heart Prairie Press, 1991).

History Learning Site. "Horses in World War One." http://www.historylearningsite.co.uk/horses_in_world_war_one.htm

Jane Austen Magazine. "Sedan Chairs." http://janeausten.co.uk/magazine/features.html?pid=296&step=4

Keegan, John. A History of Warfare. (New York: Vintage Books, 1993).

Piggott, Stuart. Wagon, Chariot, and Carriage: Symbol and Status in the History of Transport. (Slovenia: Thames and Hudson, 1992).

Reader's Digest. Story of the Great American West. (Pleasantville: Reader's Digest Association, Inc., 1977).

Smith, D.J.M. A Dictionary of Horse Drawn Vehicles. (London: Pelham Books, 1988).

Time Life Books. America's Wild West. (Alexandria: Time Life Books, 1993).

Walrond, Sallie. Looking at Carriages. (London: Pelham Books, 1980).
The Encyclopedia of Carriage Driving. (London: J.A. Allen & Co. Ltd, 1988).

Watney, Marylian. The Elegant Carriage. (London: J.A. Allen & Co. Ltd, 1979).

Weber, Phillip. They Did it With Horses. (Whitewater: Prairie Heart Press, 2000).

Made in the USA
Charleston, SC
27 September 2014